RENEE SERVELLO

BABY BARNEY
NEEDS
HUGS & FOOD!

EXPLORA BOOKS
700 – 838 West Hastings St. Vancouver, BC V6C 0A6
www.explorabooks.com
Phone: (604) 330 6795

No part of this book may be reproduced, stored in a retrieval system, or transmitted by any means without the written permission of the author.

Because of the dynamic nature of the Internet, any web addresses or links contained in this book may have changed since publication and may no longer be valid. The views expressed in this work are solely those of the author and do not necessarily reflect the views of the publisher, and the publisher hereby disclaims any responsibility for them.

ISBN: 978-1-83430-069-6 (*Paperback*)
978-183430-070-2 (*Hardback*)

© 2025 Reneé Servello. All rights reserved.

Barney is dedicated to my fantastic Brother, Cody Cotten, who is a MAJOR dog lover! He will easily identify with Barney's escapades.

Other books by Renee Servello

Petey the Pug Escapes
for 24 Hours
Freckles Finds a Forever Home
Humor All the Way
You're Kidding.. I'm A Senior?

Hi, my name is Baby Barney.
I am a Labradoodle puppy.
I may be a puppy, but I
am growing like a rocket,
no kidding.
We have a little problem.
When I was little, everyone
could pick me up, that's hard
to do now.

I keep growing and growing. I'm also getting heavier and heavier. That means that it is hard to pick me up. I also don't fit on my doggie bed now. I really don't fit on anything!

When I try to go upstairs or downstairs with my family, I accidentally bump into them, and sometimes they fall down. I think they are playing with me when that happens, but faces sorta look unhappy.

My family buys me bowls to eat out of, but they are too small. I'm getting bigger, not smaller. I think they're realizing that now because all of a sudden I have a ginormous bowl. I get full when I eat now.

When my family and I all
sit around together, I used
to lie on the couch
with them.
No more! They say,
"Sorry Barney, but you are
just too big."
Down to the floor I go,
it's sad for me.

I used to sleep on my family's beds. No more. They say, "Barney, you are too big and take up the whole bed." Down to the floor I go!

My fun comes when the school bus arrives for my family. I can go outside and wait with them for the bus.
That's really fun because sometimes the bus driver lets me go up a few steps of the bus, and the kids squeal and hug me. Now that makes me happy!

I'm big now, but I love my hugs, so if you see me outside, stop and hug me. I'll even give you you some kisses.

Guess what?
We all need to visit our doctors, so we can be well.
My doctor is called a vet, or veterinarian. He gives me dog bones. Yum!
But to be honest, it scares me half to death when we go there.
I shake and shake and can't stand up.
My family has to carry me into the office, and it's not easy because I am so big.

Sometimes my family drives our group to the beach. They even take me! What I love to do during the ride is have the window part way open so my head is in the breeze. Then I "bite the air"; boy, is that fun!

When we get out of the car at the beach, we all go into the water. Have you ever chased after real, live fish in the ocean? Now THAT is fun, but I've never caught one yet. Fish know how to swim really fast. They are just too fast for Barney.

Do you know how to swim?
Summertime is really fun;
but take swimming lessons if
you are going to the
beach or swimming pool.
My family let's me get in
the pools because
they know that I can swim.
I'm pretty big,
but I learned how to swim
when I was a puppy.
You can learn too, it's fun.

Another thing that happens at my house is that the postman comes every day. He is my best friend, he brings me treats - IF I don't knock him down! He really doesn't like it when I sit on him. It is sorta funny though.

I may be big, but everyone loves me. I don't fit in anyone's lap now, but I have a ton of fun with my family. Barney is no longer Baby Barney. I'm just Barney since I grew up. I am loved and happy. But don't forget that I still want more food, I'm always hungry.
Love you,
Barney

Renee' Servello is a wife, mother, grandmother and a great grandmother.
She has given children the delightful book
Petey the Pug Escapes for 24 Hours.
Her most recent book is
Baby Barney needs Hugs & Food!
Another thoroughly exciting story of a Labradoodle dog and its journey growing up with its family.

www.ingramcontent.com/pod-product-compliance
Lightning Source LLC
Chambersburg PA
CBRC091206070526
44584CB00008B/336